ULYSSES S. GRANT

The Presidents of the United States

George Washington
1789–1797

John Adams
1797–1801

Thomas Jefferson
1801–1809

James Madison
1809–1817

James Monroe
1817–1825

John Quincy Adams
1825–1829

Andrew Jackson
1829–1837

Martin Van Buren
1837–1841

William Henry Harrison
1841

John Tyler
1841–1845

James Polk
1845–1849

Zachary Taylor
1849–1850

Millard Fillmore
1850–1853

Franklin Pierce
1853–1857

James Buchanan
1857–1861

Abraham Lincoln
1861–1865

Andrew Johnson
1865–1869

Ulysses S. Grant
1869–1877

Rutherford B. Hayes
1877–1881

James Garfield
1881

Chester Arthur
1881–1885

Grover Cleveland
1885–1889

Benjamin Harrison
1889–1893

Grover Cleveland
1893–1897

William McKinley
1897–1901

Theodore Roosevelt
1901–1909

William H. Taft
1909–1913

Woodrow Wilson
1913–1921

Warren Harding
1921–1923

Calvin Coolidge
1923–1929

Herbert Hoover
1929–1933

Franklin D. Roosevelt
1933–1945

Harry Truman
1945–1953

Dwight Eisenhower
1953–1961

John F. Kennedy
1961–1963

Lyndon Johnson
1963–1969

Richard Nixon
1969–1974

Gerald Ford
1974–1977

Jimmy Carter
1977–1981

Ronald Reagan
1981–1989

George H. W. Bush
1989–1993

William J. Clinton
1993–2001

George W. Bush
2001–present

Presidents and Their Times

ULYSSES S. GRANT

BILLY ARONSON

Marshall Cavendish
Benchmark
New York

Marshall Cavendish Benchmark
99 White Plains Road
Tarrytown, NY 10591-9001
www.marshallcavendish.us

Library of Congress Cataloging-in-Publication Data
Aronson, Billy.
Ulysses S. Grant / by Billy Aronson.
p. cm. — (Presidents and their times)
Summary: "This series provides comprehensive information on the presidents of the United States and places each within his historical and cultural context; it also explores the formative events of his times and how he responds"—Provided by publisher.
Includes bibliographical references and index.
ISBN-13: 978-0-7614-2430-7
1. Grant, Ulysses S. (Ulysses Simpson), 1822–1885—Juvenile literature. 2. Presidents—United States—Biography—Juvenile literature. 3. Generals—United States—Biography—Juvenile literature. 4. United States. Army—Biography—Juvenile literature. I. Title. II. Series.
E672.A77 2007
973.8'2092—dc22 [B] 2006011087

Editor: Christine Florie
Publisher: Michelle Bisson
Editorial Director: Michelle Bisson
Art Director: Anahid Hamparian
Series Designer: Alex Ferrari

Photo research by Connie Gardner

Cover Photo by Bettmann/CORBIS

The photographs in this book are used by permission and courtesy of: *The Granger Collection*: 3, 9, 15, 17, 25, 33, 39, 43, 50, 67, 76, 81. *Corbis*: 6, 8, 53; Royalty Free, 2; Samuel Sartain, 14; Bettmann, 29, 37, 60, 75; Medford Historical Society Collection, 34; Poodles Rock, 40; James Leynse, 78. *Brown Brothers*: 18, 24, 72. *North Wind Picture Archives*: 19, 45, 55, 63, 64. *Getty Images*: Photo by MPI, 12, 28: Hulton Archive, 47; Library of Congress, 49. *Art Resource*: National Portrait Gallery, Smithsonian Institution/Art Resource, NY, 22, 61.

Printed in Malaysia
1 3 5 6 4 2

CONTENTS

Record numbers of Americans came to see the inauguration of war hero Ulysses S. Grant.

Youth

One

On March 4, 1869, Americans from across the United States gathered in Washington, D.C., to see the **inauguration** of the eighteenth president. Inauguration ceremonies had always been well attended. But more people had come to watch this president take office than any before him—and with good reason: the nation was on shaky ground. It had just survived the bloodiest war in its history, the Civil War, which tore the nation in half. During that bitter war, members of some families had even taken arms against one another. The peace that followed was hardly calm. In parts of the country, angry mobs burned down homes and schools, and charged through the streets murdering people. The outgoing president, Andrew Johnson, was so hated by leaders in Congress that they tried to throw him out of office. The president before Johnson, Abraham Lincoln, had been murdered. To many citizens it seemed that the nation was again at war with itself.

On this day, though, there was hope. The newly elected president was admired by people across the country. He wasn't particularly tall or muscular, and a thick black beard covered much of his face. But it wasn't his looks that inspired awe; it was his proven ability to get people working together. The hope that he could encourage Americans to work together had motivated voters to elect him to the highest office in the land. Now, as he walked down the steps of the Capitol in his fine black suit, all eyes were focused on the general about to become president, Ulysses S. Grant.

As far as the public was concerned, Grant's rise to fame had been swift. Seven years earlier no one had heard of him. For

Grant himself, however, the path had been long and difficult. There had been pain, disappointment, and humiliation along the way. At every step, though, Grant had been learning.

Childhood

Ulysses Grant was born on April 27, 1822, in the quiet village of Point Pleasant, Ohio. At that time the United States was a rural country made up of some two dozen states. People weren't really sure just how united these states actually were. Many thought of the states as independent bodies that would work together when it was convenient, such as when fighting a common enemy, but were always free to leave if they so desired. Others felt that the states were permanently linked as a nation. In half of the states, it was legal for one person to own another. According to the rules of slavery, white people could buy and sell black people.

During his presidency, Grant was often visited by his father, but his mother never came to the White House.

Ulysses's father, Jesse Root Grant, was a farmer and a tanner. Working in a tannery behind their house, Jesse Grant prepared leather goods to sell to the many pioneers who passed through Ohio on their way westward. A hardworking self-made businessman, Jesse Grant loved his country and hated slavery. Ulysses's mother,

Hannah Simpson Grant, was an extremely quiet woman who never showed emotion. Ulysses would one day admit to a friend, "I never once saw my mother cry." Historians believe Grant received his hatred of slavery from his father and his tendency to hide his feelings from his mother.

The Oldest of Six

When Ulysses was born, Hannah and Jesse Grant lived in a two-room cabin in Point Pleasant, Ohio (below). After a year the three moved to a bigger house in nearby Georgetown, where the family grew to include two more boys and three girls.

At the age of three Ulysses revealed a passion that took his parents by surprise. When a traveling circus came to town, a performer asked if anyone wanted to ride the pony. Little Ulysses begged to be chosen and was placed on the pony's back. To the crowd's amazement the toddler rode the pony, holding on tightly to its mane, totally delighted with himself. In the years ahead Ulysses would show an intense love for horses and stunning skill in riding them.

At around the same time an older boy decided to subject Ulysses to a cruel test. Ulysses had never heard a gunshot blast. The older boy was curious to see how Ulysses would react. When the boy held the gun near Ulysses's head, pointing it away, and fired, Ulysses didn't even flinch! Years later, in battle, Ulysses would show the same amazing ability to remain cool as missiles exploded all around him.

Another unusual trait of young Ulysses was his unwillingness to retrace his steps. If he ever happened to pass a street where he should have turned, he would keep going forward and go all the way around the block, rather than turn back. His refusal to retreat would one day inspire an army—and preserve a nation.

In school Ulysses was considered shy, though not unfriendly. As one girl described it, "He was a real nice boy who never had anything to say, and when he said anything he always said it short." At home he disliked helping out his father in the tannery because Ulysses was disgusted by the sight and smell of the skins of dead animals. He made up for this by being a great help on the farm, where he drove the horses that were pulling carts and hauling tools and equipment. Ulysses soon earned a reputation for breaking in unruly horses. Combining patience and firmness, the boy could tame any horse. Eventually Ulysses figured out a way to use this skill to make money: he set up a frontier limousine service and taxied customers around in a horse-drawn carriage.

Unfortunately, dealing with money was never his specialty. Once, when Ulysses was about eight years old, he wanted to purchase a horse from a neighbor, so his businessman father tried to coach Ulysses on how to negotiate. The neighbor was asking $25 for the horse, so Jesse Grant advised his son to start out by offering $20. If that offer was refused, he should offer $22.50. If that, too, was refused he should pay the full $25. When Ulysses went to buy the horse, he remembered his father's words—but delivered them all at once! He told the man he planned to offer $20 and then $22.50 and then $25. Not surprisingly, the man

Sam I Am?

While growing up, Grant was known to friends and family by many names. At birth he was named Hiram Ulysses Grant, the middle name honoring the Greek mythical warrior Ulysses. When he was a child, schoolmates who mistook his quietness for stupidity nicknamed him Useless Grant. When he went away to college at West Point he felt ashamed of his initials H. U. G., so he reversed Hiram and Ulysses to yield Ulysses Hiram Grant. An official mistakenly assumed his middle name was his mother's maiden name and enrolled him as Ulysses S. Grant. Grant noticed that this change made his first two initials those of his country. So did his West Point classmates, who called him United States Grant, and then Uncle Sam Grant, and then simply, Sam.

took the full $25 and informed Jesse of his son's negotiating blunder. Clearly the boy didn't have the patience for business that he had for horses.

Military School

When it was time to choose a career, Ulysses knew only that he definitely didn't want to work in his father's tannery. Jesse didn't know what to do with his son until he heard about an opening at West Point, the national military academy in New York State. Besides offering a great education, West Point was free. Ulysses had no interest in going to military school. He hated the noise and pomp of military parades and would rather farm than fight. But his father insisted that Ulysses was going to West Point, so he went.

During his four years at West Point, Ulysses grew 6 inches, from 5'1" to 5'7". His academic growth was less obvious. He did well in math, his best subject. He also enjoyed art class, in which his keen eye for detail enabled him to create some impressive paintings. He preferred reading novels to doing homework, however, so it's no surprise that his grades were only average. Socially he was timid—he didn't go to parties or play sports.

Upon graduating, Grant didn't get any special honors, but he played a starring role in the riding show that was the highlight of the graduation ceremony. The riding master raised the jumping bar higher than a man's height and called Grant forward. Mounted on a massive horse named York, Grant prepared to

Though Grant wasn't interested in a military career, his father's efforts landed him an appointment at West Point.

attempt a stunt so difficult that some of his friends feared he might be killed. As the crowd watched in awe, he charged ahead on York so smoothly that, according to one observer, it seemed "as if man and beast were welded together." At just the right moment the two leaped, cleared the hurdle, and set a West Point record that went unbroken for twenty-five years.

After leaving West Point, Grant hoped to find a job as a math professor. While waiting for a teaching job, he did what most military school graduates do, he accepted a position in the army. For Ulysses this meant serving as a second lieutenant at a base in St. Louis, Missouri. Though little happened in St. Louis that would have a lasting affect on Grant, something happened nearby that would change him forever.

Courtship

One day Grant went to visit the family of an old college friend, Fred Dent, at a farm called White Haven. Fred's father, Frederick, was a slave owner who loved to preach proslavery views. Although Grant disliked listening to Frederick Dent's opinions, in the months ahead he found himself returning to the Dents' home again and again. He wasn't coming to see his friend Fred or to argue with Fred's father, but to see Fred's younger sister, Julia.

At seventeen, Julia was nearly four years younger than Ulysses. She was cross-eyed, but she was also witty, smart, and optimistic. Her lively personality won the timid soldier's heart. Together the two would go walking or riding; Julia's horse was one of the few that could keep up with Ulysses's.

When he learned that his company was to be moved to Louisiana, Ulysses hurried to White Haven to present Julia with his

Julia Dent won Grant's heart with her spirit and wit, and the two later married.

class ring. Julia understood that this was Ulysses's way of asking her to marry him—he couldn't bring himself to say the words. She decided to refuse the ring, claiming that her mother wouldn't let her accept expensive gifts. After Ulysses left feeling wounded and rejected, Julia found herself missing her suitor terribly. She had dreams about him. She even named the post on her new bed Ulysses. As the days passed, she wondered if she would ever see him again.

But Ulysses Grant wasn't about to give up the fight. Before leaving for Louisiana, he returned to White Haven and took Julia for a ride in a borrowed carriage. As they rode, Julia noticed that Ulysses was being unusually quiet. When he drove the carriage over a small bridge, the stream below was so swollen that water began to lap at their shoes. Julia took the opportunity to cling to her driver. "Now if anything happens," she said, "I shall cling to you, no matter what you say." Ulysses thought for a moment. Then he seized the opening. Would she like to cling to him *forever*? he asked. Julia answered that she would. He offered her the ring again, and this time she accepted. Working together, they had achieved a major victory.

Over the years Julia would indeed cling to Ulysses and he to her. At first they would have to do their clinging in secret,

Grant proposed marriage to Julia Dent during a carriage ride.

though. Julia wanted time to convince her father that Ulysses was worthy. But their courtship would take longer than either had imagined, as the couple's desire for marriage was interrupted by their nation's desire for more land.

War and Work — Two

Today many historians see the Mexican War as an act of American aggression. Americans wanted to take Texas and other southwestern territory from Mexico, so they did. One idea that inspired this aggression was the concept of **manifest destiny**. According to this concept, it was the country's manifest destiny, or obvious fate, to expand westward until it reached from sea to shining sea. To pioneers the west seemed like a wilderness waiting to be tamed by fearless settlers. But to those already living in the west, such as Native Americans and Mexicans, manifest destiny was a fancy phrase for stealing land.

Even back then, some Americans saw the Mexican War as unfair. Congressman Abraham Lincoln spoke against it. Grant himself would later write that the war was "one of the most unjust ever waged by a stronger against a weaker nation." But the man elected president in 1844, James K. Polk, saw things differently. A devout believer in manifest destiny, Polk was determined to expand the country in any way he could. On June 29, 1845, he ordered General Zachary Taylor to lead a battalion of troops, which included Grant, into southwestern territory that belonged to Mexico. Though Polk claimed this was to protect American settlers living there, it had the effect of provoking war. When the Mexican cavalry eventually stood up to the American troops, the war began.

Grant's First War

Though Grant had studied all about war at West Point, it wasn't until the Mexican War that he got his first sight of bloodshed—and it sickened him. After a brief battle at Palo Alto, a salt prairie in Texas, Grant walked over the battlefield and was devastated. "It was a terrible sight," he observed, "to see the amount of life that had been destroyed. The ground was strewn with dead men and horses." As other soldiers celebrated because the battle had been won, Grant felt only sorrow for the dead on both sides. He felt disgust as well, as he disclosed in letters to friends in which he described an American captain's injury. "A shot knocked the lower jaw of Captain Page entirely away," Grant wrote. "The lower jaw is gone to the wind pipe and the tongue hangs down upon the throat. He will never be able to speak or eat."

Grant had his first taste of war at the Battle of Palo Alto on May 8, 1846.

As quartermaster of his regiment, Grant refused to remain behind the lines of battle and often rushed to the front lines.

Besides learning about bloodshed, Grant learned about inspiring leadership during the Mexican War by observing General Taylor. Nicknamed Old Rough and Ready, Taylor didn't make a fuss about fancy uniforms or military parades. His boots were often covered with mud and his jacket was wrinkled. But he spoke to the soldiers as though they were his friends, and they respected him in return. Grant also admired Taylor's ability to give orders simply and clearly, to do the best with what he had, and to stay calm and confident in battle. "These qualities are more rarely found than genius or physical courage," Grant noted.

As Taylor's troops moved deeper into Mexico, Grant was given the position of **quartermaster**. This meant he would oversee the mules carrying the army's food and ammunition. Being quartermaster was something of an honor; Grant's notable skill working with horses was the main reason he was chosen. But Grant didn't want to be kept in the back with the mules while his comrades faced danger on the front line. So when a battle began, he often made his way into the thick of the fight.

During an intense battle in the Mexican city of Monterrey, Grant volunteered for an especially dangerous mission. Someone was needed to carry an urgent request for more weapons through the town, which was heavily guarded by Mexican soldiers. To stay safe from enemy fire, Grant clung to the side of his gray horse, Nelly, with his arms around her neck and one foot around the saddle. Like a rodeo rider doing a stunt, Grant thundered through the streets hanging off Nelly's side, up one street, down another, as snipers' bullets whizzed by. After his mission was accomplished, the modest hero suggested that Nelly had shown more courage than he.

Of Grant's breathtaking ride for ammunitions he wrote in his memoirs, "It was only at street crossings that my horse was under fire. . . . I crossed at such a flying rate. . . . I got out safely and without a scratch."

Letting Off Smoke

In Mexico, when the pressures of war started to weigh upon Grant, he found he could relieve his stress by smoking. Though he sometimes smoked a pipe, cigars were his favorite. During the Civil War he smoked as many as twenty cigars a day. He continued to smoke cigars throughout his presidency, as well. In the end, Grant's reliance on smoking took its toll. In his early sixties Grant developed throat cancer that proved fatal; the great general who survived several of America's bloodiest battles was killed by tobacco.

When President Polk grew restless with how the war was going, he replaced Taylor with General Winfield Scott. Old Fuss and Feathers, as Scott was called, was the opposite of Taylor in many ways. While Taylor was plain and humble, Scott was a fancy and formal man, who decked out his uniform with as many badges and decorations as possible. But Grant found that he had as much to learn from his new leader as he had from the last.

One thing Grant learned from General Scott was that an army could survive while cut off from its **supply line**. Traditionally, an army moving into enemy territory would keep a path open leading back to friendly territory. This path, called a supply line, allowed an army to keep getting food and ammunition. As Scott led his troops deep into Mexico he abandoned the supply line connecting them to the United States, and had them live off the land, eating whatever they could hunt, pick off trees, or buy. In this way they could move boldly toward the enemy, while eating just fine.

In the last major battle for Mexico City, Grant combined courage and courtesy to help achieve victory. At one point he needed to enter a church in order to haul a cannon up to the belfry to fire down on enemy troops. The church door had been bolted shut, however, and the priest inside refused to open up. As the battle raged, Grant reasoned politely with the priest through a peephole. If the priest didn't open the door, Grant would have to destroy it, he explained, which wouldn't do anyone any good. The priest listened to reason and opened the door, allowing Grant to charge up and fire down, helping to bring a quick American victory.

Marriage

When Mexico surrendered, the United States gained new territory extending from Texas to California. Grant was promoted to first lieutenant, and, as soon as he could, he applied for leave and returned to Julia. The three years apart had made the couple's hearts grow fonder. Julia's father had grown fonder of Grant, too—he now regarded Grant as a war hero. On August 22, 1848, in a joyous ceremony at the Dents' house, Ulysses and Julia were finally married.

While many officers left the army after the war, Grant decided to stay on. Though he found the peacetime army dull, it was steady work that paid well. After serving at one army base in Detroit, Michigan, he was assigned to another in Sackett's Harbor, New York. In the second year of their marriage, Julia gave birth to their first child, Fred.

After two years Grant was separated from his little family when his army company was relocated to California. Since 1848, when gold was discovered in California, people from all over the

Feeling homesick and unhappy on the West Coast, Grant wrote Julia, "How broken I feel here."

country had been heading west hoping to get rich. As this gold rush continued, soldiers such as Grant were needed on the West Coast to keep law and order. Though Julia wanted to go with him, Grant refused to let her make the difficult trip, because she was pregnant with their second child. Grant decided that he would go west by himself and be joined by Julia and the children at a later day.

But that day never came. What did come was one of the darkest periods in Grant's life. Even after he was promoted to captain, Grant did not earn enough money on the West Coast to have his family join him there, and he was miserable without them. Though he'd been a loner growing up, after a taste of marriage he found being alone unbearable. So Grant decided to try to make more money any way he could.

Everything he tried failed. He opened a store with a friend, but the friend took Grant's money and fled. Then he tried selling cattle and hogs with a partner, but this business only lost money. When Grant heard that ice was selling for high prices in San Francisco, he bought 100 tons of ice and put it on a boat headed for northern California, but a strong wind delayed the boat's arrival and the ice melted. Next he decided to sell chickens in San Francisco, but the boat carrying the chickens was delayed and the chickens died. He and a partner then opened a club where soldiers could relax, but the man Grant hired to run the club stole their money. His partner in this business observed that Grant was so kind and honest he believed everybody else to be honest, too. He was no more shrewd than he had been as a boy, when he "negotiated" the purchase of a horse by announcing the top price he could pay right off the bat. Somehow, in war Grant was able to size up a situation, make quick decisions, and learn from his mistakes. In business, though, he kept making the same mistakes over and over again.

Letters from home brought Grant cheer. As he wrote to Julia, "When I got these letters I jumped with joy. You have no idea how happy it made me feel." But over time the letters made Grant frustrated, especially after he learned of the birth of his second child, a boy named after him. "I would prefer sacrificing my commission and try[ing] something [else] to continuing this separation," he wrote. "If I could see Fred and hear him talk, and see little Ulys, I could then be contented provided their mother was with them."

Mrs. Ulysses S. Grant poses for a photograph with her two eldest children Fred (right) and Ulysses S. Jr. about 1854.

As the months passed, Grant became so sad and lonely that he turned to alcohol for solace. Though the other soldiers drank heavily, Grant didn't handle his liquor as well as most. Several mouthfuls made him slur his words. A drink or two made him completely drunk. In the spring of 1854, Grant suddenly resigned from the army, claiming it was because he missed his family. There were rumors that Grant had been asked to resign after being found drunk on the job.

MONEY PROBLEMS

In order to support his family, Grant took up farming.

Grant was thrilled to return to Julia and the boys. Without his army job, however, his money problems only got worse. Julia's father had given them a farm near St. Louis as a wedding present, so Grant tried to support his family by farming. As Grant built up the farm, the couple continued building their family. Julia gave birth to a girl named Nellie, and then to their fourth and last child, a boy named Jesse. Eventually Grant was able to raise fine crops of potatoes, cabbage, and melons. But just then, the country was hit by a **depression**, and no one could afford to buy the crops. At Christmas, Grant had to sell his gold watch so he could afford to buy presents for his children. The next year the economy improved, but Grant's crops were destroyed by an unusually cold summer followed by an early frost. The only things left on the farm were trees. So Grant chopped them down, hauled the logs into town, and stood on a street corner trying to sell firewood.

He got a job selling real estate. Sadly, he wasn't shrewd enough to be a good salesman. He tried collecting rents, but he was too nice to demand that people pay. He secured a customhouse job for two months in 1859, but lost it when the collector of customs died. At around this time Grant was given a slave. Though Grant could have sold the slave for one thousand dollars—enough to support his family for a year—he set the slave free. Grant refused to treat another person as property to be bought and sold, even in his desperate state.

And Grant was desperate. A friend who saw him on the street observed, "I had never before seen him so depressed. He was shabbily dressed, his beard unshorn, his face anxious." Finally, Grant had no choice but to ask his father for a job in the family business. Though in the past Jesse Grant had ignored his son's requests for help, this time he said yes.

So in April 1860 Ulysses and family left St. Louis for Galena, Illinois, where Jesse Grant had set up a leather goods store run by Ulysses's brothers. Grant was content to work as a clerk, pay off his debts, and keep his family together—until the United States started coming apart.

BECOMING A GENERAL *Three*

Throughout the 1800s the United States was looking more and more like two separate nations moving in two different ways. In the North industry was booming and slavery was illegal. In the South the economy was based on farming and depended on slavery.

As the country expanded westward, Northerners felt slavery should be kept out of the new territories. Southerners passionately disagreed. Politicians made compromises to keep both sides happy. By 1860, when Abraham Lincoln was elected president, Southerners had had enough. Since Lincoln belonged to the antislavery **Republican Party**, Southerners felt that the new president's sympathies threatened their way of life. They decided it was time for the southern states to leave the Union.

From time to time in the nation's history, individual states had talked about "seceding," or leaving the Union. The reason they felt they had a right to **secede** was simple: each state had joined the nation by choice. So why couldn't a state also choose to leave? There were people both in the North and in the South who felt the South had a right to secede. They were called **secessionists**.

But there were also those across the country who disagreed. **Unionists**, as these patriots were called, felt that the alliance between the states was permanent and that no state could leave. Some Unionists believed that national unity had been permanent from the moment the states joined together. Others felt that it had become permanent over time, as the states worked together to build the nation over the years. Abraham Lincoln was a Unionist. So was Ulysses Grant.

When President Lincoln took office, he forbade southern states from leaving the Union, to no avail. Seven southern states (South Carolina, Mississippi, Florida, Alabama, Georgia, Louisiana, and Texas) seceded and formed a new nation where slavery would always be legal. They called this nation the Confederate States of America, or simply the **Confederacy**. Since they were rebelling against the Union, members of the Confederacy were called rebels. The Civil War began on April 12, 1861, when rebels fired on Union soldiers in South Carolina's Fort Sumter. At once, four more southern states (Virginia, Arkansas, Tennessee, and North Carolina) seceded, too, bringing the total number of Confederate states to eleven.

The Confederate attack on Fort Sumter in Charleston Harbor, South Carolina, marked the beginning of the Civil War.

Back in the Army

As soon as war broke out, Grant began applying for an appointment as an officer in the Union army. He approached army friends for help and wrote letters to prominant officials, but nothing seemed to work. Maybe Grant was passed over because of rumors of his past drunkenness. He may have lost out because he did not brag. In one letter applying for a position he described himself simply as "competent." Or maybe the problem was his appearance—slouching and scruffy, Grant didn't look like a leader.

Combining natural talent and skill with lessons he learned from generals he admired, Grant proved to be an effective leader in battle.

While waiting for an assignment, Grant accepted a job training local volunteers. Using the same combination of strictness and patience with which he broke in horses, Grant transformed farm boys into soldiers. Eventually a position with the army did come through: Grant was made colonel of a regiment in Illinois.

Many of Grant's West Point classmates started out with higher ranks than he. Some began the war as generals. But starting with a lower rank would prove to work in Grant's favor. It allowed him to develop his leadership skills gradually, taking risks, and learning from his mistakes, one step at a time. As Grant grew into a great leader, the number of men in his command increased. So did the importance of his missions.

Grant's on-the-job training began when he led his regiment of 1,250 men toward a rebel camp in Missouri led by Confederate Colonel Thomas Harris. As a soldier in Mexico, Grant had risked his own life, but this was the first time Grant might be leading other men to their deaths. That thought terrified him. He would later recall:

> *As we approached the brow of the hill from which it was expected we could see Harris' camp, and possibly find his men ready formed to meet us, my heart kept getting higher and higher until it felt to me as though it was in my throat. I would have given anything then to have been back in Illinois.*

In spite of his feelings, he kept going. Finally Grant reached the top of the hill, looked down, and saw something amazing: the rebels had fled! As scared as Grant had been, his enemy had been even more scared. His discovery that the enemy could be as terrified as he was served as a precious lesson Grant would never forget. From then on he would take advantage of his enemy's fear—and ignore his own.

Forts Henry and Donelson

As Grant's leadership skills became recognized, he was promoted to brigadier general. In this new position he had a chance to plan bold ways to attack the enemy. In early 1862 Grant approached

Taylor-Made

As Grant led troops into battle, he displayed many of the qualities he had admired in General Zachary Taylor. Like Taylor, Grant's humble appearance and kind manner won the total devotion of his men. Like Taylor, the younger officer never complained to his superiors about the difficulty of a task he was assigned to carry out. Also like Taylor, Grant had a remarkable ability to communicate clearly with his troops. As another Union general's chief of staff said of Grant's orders,

No matter how hurriedly he may write them on the field, no one ever has the slightest doubt as to their meaning, or even has to read them over a second time to understand him.

Even amid the noise and confusion of battle, Grant could instruct men where to go and what to do when they got there, in such a way that no one was confused. This ability would bring success to Grant, as it had to his mentor.

the general above him, Henry Halleck, with his boldest idea yet: Grant wanted to attack Fort Henry and Fort Donelson. Located on the southern border of Kentucky, these forts gave the rebels a strong hold on the state. Without them, the northern army could control Kentucky and move into Tennessee. Grant believed that if he attacked at once, before the rebels could build up their strength in these forts, he could take them both. At first Halleck thought Grant's plan too risky. President Lincoln was pressuring Halleck to be more aggressive, however, so Halleck approved Grant's plan.

The first part of Grant's plan went smoothly. As Union navy gunboats blasted Fort Henry from the Tennessee River, the defenders surrendered quickly. Part two would be more difficult though. Fort Donelson was higher up, on a hill, so it would be harder to attack. Moreover, it was better constructed than Fort Henry. The defenders would be better prepared since they had learned of the attack on Fort Henry. Grant's men would be deeper into enemy territory, and they would be outnumbered.

Halleck wanted Grant to wait for reinforcements before attacking. Grant, though, was in no mood to wait. He remembered how Generals Taylor and Scott had defeated bigger armies deep in Mexico by being aggressive. "I was very impatient to get to Fort Donelson because I knew the importance of the place to the enemy," Grant would later write, "and supposed he would reinforce it rapidly. I felt that 15,000 men on the 8th would be more effective than 50,000 a month later." Above all, Grant wanted to keep the momentum. So on he led.

The battle for Fort Donelson didn't begin well for Grant. When his troops tried to attack the fort, they were driven back by the rebels. Navy gunboats that tried to shell the fort from the nearby Cumberland River did little damage. As night fell, the temperature dropped and freezing rain turned to snow. While his men tried to get some sleep outside the fort, Grant went to the Cumberland River to meet with the navy commander, some distance away.

Meanwhile, inside the fort, the sleepless rebels came up with a plan: they would break out of the fort before dawn, taking Union troops by surprise. When Grant returned to his men in the early afternoon, he found that the battle had begun without him. Hundreds of his men had been killed or wounded. Some Union soldiers panicked, running around in all directions. No captains were giving orders, for many had no idea of what to do.

But Grant did have an idea. When he noticed that rebel soldiers were wearing their knapsacks, he took that to mean they were thinking of fleeing and not coming back. This told Grant that deep down the rebels felt they couldn't hold the fort. So Grant commanded his men to stand firm. He ordered them to

While other Union generals were experiencing defeat, Grant's success at the Battle of Fort Donelson in Tennessee earned him hero status in the North.

FRIENDS AND ENEMIES

Grant's demand for unconditional surrender at Donelson would have struck any opponent at that time as rude. But General Buckner (below) was especially surprised to receive such harsh terms, since he and Grant were friends! They had met some twenty years earlier at West Point. Buckner had even lent Grant money when Grant resigned from the army and couldn't afford the trip home. After Buckner surrendered, Grant remembered his friend's kindness and offered to give the defeated general any cash he might need.

load their weapons, form a line, surround the escaping soldiers, and attack. "This worked like a charm," Grant observed. "The men only wanted someone to give them a command."

When the Confederate commander, General Simon Bolivar Buckner, asked Grant for his terms of surrender, he received a harsh reply: Grant would accept nothing but "**unconditional surrender**." Buckner was taken aback by Grant's demand, calling it "ungenerous and unchivalrous." In those days, it was considered courteous for a winning officer to offer the loser a deal of some kind. But General Grant wasn't making any deals. The rebels simply had to give up—and do so at once.

With the surrender of Fort Donelson, the Union won thousands of Confederate guns, thousands of horses, and more than 14,000 prisoners—the most that had ever been captured in an American battle. Though Grant had been ruthless in demanding surrender, after the rebels yielded Grant showed kindness. He fed them, let them keep their personal belongings, and let them tend to their wounded. He also saw to it that the defeated men were treated with respect. Years of personal failure had taught Grant the pain of being humiliated. So he refused to let his men celebrate where the rebels could hear.

Throughout the North, though, there was celebration. Church bells rang. People danced in the streets cheering the first Union victory—and the hero of that victory, Brigadier General Ulysses S. Grant. When word spread that Grant smoked cigars, adoring Northerners sent him countless boxes of cigars. Grant was also given a new nickname: Unconditional Surrender Grant. No one was calling him Useless now.

Shiloh

With Kentucky under Union control, General Halleck sent Grant into Tennessee with 36,000 troops. There Grant was to wait for more Union soldiers to arrive before moving on to attack the Confederate army at Corinth. While waiting in the town of Pittsburg Landing near a church called Shiloh, Grant had his troops spend a lot of time exercising. He didn't bother to have them dig trenches in which they could defend themselves, since he thought the enemy wouldn't dare attack. He was wrong.

On the morning of April 6, 1862, Grant's troops suddenly found tens of thousands of Confederate troops charging through the woods, set to kill them. Seized by terror, Union soldiers scattered. Grant would later recall, "Many of the regiments broke at the first fire. . . . Colonels led their regiments from the field on first hearing the whistle of the enemy's bullets. . . . Men fled panic stricken." Many of those who did stand and fight were killed or captured. The Union was on the brink of a humiliating defeat.

Grant refused to let that happen. With his troops panicking all around him, he was able to remain calm and size up the situation. Observing where most of the bullets were coming from, he formed new battle lines and inspired his men to stand firm. For two days the armies clashed. The air was filled with the sound of cannons blasting and swarms of bullets being fired. The green fields were blanketed with blood and corpses.

When the battle called Shiloh was over, it was hard to say who really had won. Southern troops stumbled away, too tired to run. Northern troops let them go, too exhausted to chase. In two days of fighting, over 23,000 men had been killed, wounded, or captured—more than had been lost in all American wars up to that point. In the North newspapers blamed Grant for leaving his men open to attack in the first place. One writer claimed that "the loss of life was terrific and seems wholly caused by bad management in the field, or no management at all." Some politicians insisted Grant should be fired. But the president disagreed. "I can't spare this man," Abraham Lincoln said. "He fights!"

"He fights" might seem like small praise for a soldier, but Lincoln meant it as a serious compliment. The other generals he had been using were in no hurry to face the enemy. When Lincoln ordered his generals to attack, they would take their time

The Sensitive Soldier

Though Grant was tough and fearless in warfare, between battles he was sensitive and shy. He wouldn't share a tent because he didn't want to change in front of other men. He wouldn't let anyone tell off-color jokes in his presence. His concern for the suffering of animals made it difficult for him to eat meat. As his lieutenant colonel Horace Porter remembered:

About the only meat he enjoyed was beef, and this he could not eat unless it was so thoroughly well done that no appearance of blood could be seen. If blood appeared on any meat which came on the table the sight of it seemed entirely to destroy his appetite.

The general couldn't stand the sight of blood.

or ignore him completely. Committed to the traditional style of warfare, these generals would try to intimidate an enemy with clever strategies and shows of power while avoiding direct confrontation at all costs. But Lincoln could tell that Grant was different. He felt Grant's aggressive spirit was exactly what was needed to beat the rebels. The following year proved him right.

Vicksburg

Vicksburg, Mississippi, is a town on a cliff overlooking the Mississippi River. No precious metal was mined there, and no valuable goods were manufactured there. Because of its strategic location, however, to Union leaders it was one of the most important cities in the world. As long as Confederate troops controlled Vicksburg, the Confederacy controlled travel along the Mississippi, the mighty river that ran down the middle of the Confederacy. If the Union could capture Vicksburg and control the Mississippi, the Confederacy would be sliced in half.

In late 1862 Grant led attacks against Vicksburg and was driven back. In the spring of 1863 he tried again. Grant and his men went up and down that winding, mile-wide river, attacking Vicksburg from one point and then another. Every single time they tried, they were blasted back by Confederate cannons.

Finally Grant had an idea that was original—and risky. He decided to lead his men, along the opposite banks of the river, below Vicksburg, then cross the river and march back up behind the defenders so that he could attack from dry land. In a sense he would be trying to sneak up on the city from behind. He would be cut off from his supply line. He knew, however, that leaving the supply line had worked for Winfield Scott in Mexico, and Grant believed it would work for him now.

President Abraham Lincoln called Grant's siege of Vicksburg "one of the most brilliant in the world."

As he led most of his troops down from Vicksburg, Grant ordered other Union soldiers to attack the town from different points on the river to distract and confuse the defenders. It worked. Grant's troops made it safely ashore and caught the rebels off guard. Soon it was the rebels who were in need of food and supplies, for Grant had them trapped in the city. Day after day Grant bombarded Vicksburg until Confederate soldiers and citizens alike were hungry and exhausted. On July 4, 1863, the rebels surrendered. The Confederacy was cut in half. It was the beginning of the end for the South.

Top General

After pulling off this impressive victory, Grant was promoted to major general. A few months later, after Grant chased the

While meeting with President Abraham Lincoln, Grant found he had many admirers in Washington.

Meeting of President LINCOLN
and Gen'l GRANT.

Confederates out of Tennessee, he was promoted yet again. He was made lieutenant general, the highest rank any American soldier had held since George Washington. And he was put in charge of the entire United States Army—some 500,000 men.

President Lincoln and Grant finally met when the president called his new top general to the White House. "Why, here is General Grant," Lincoln said, smiling and offering his hand. "Well, this is a great pleasure, I assure you." After the men shook hands a crowd of officials and White House guests gathered around Grant, who began to sweat and "blush like a schoolgirl," one official noted. Cheers of "Grant, Grant, Grant" rose up. As the crowd grew, Secretary of State William Seward urged Grant to get up onto the sofa so those in the back could see him. When Grant took this advice, the screaming got even louder. One newsman wrote that it was the only "real mob" he had ever seen in the White House. "For once at least the President of the United States was not the chief figure of the picture," the writer continued. "The little, scared-looking man who stood on the crimson-covered sofa was the idol of the hour." In three eventful years Ulysses S. Grant had gone from selling firewood on a street corner to commanding the most powerful army on earth.

Let Us Have Peace *Four*

Once Grant was in charge, he came up with a strategy for winning the war that divided the Union army into two main parts. One part would head down through Georgia, deep into the South, toward the important rail center of Atlanta. This force would be led by William Tecumseh Sherman, a general whose daring Grant admired. Meanwhile, the other part of the army would head toward the Confederate capital of Richmond, Virginia. Grant himself would oversee this mission, going head-to-head with the top Confederate general, Robert E. Lee.

Grant Versus Lee

Lee and Grant were opposites in many ways. Unlike Grant, Lee was tall, handsome, and wealthy. While Grant had been unknown until recently, Lee had been celebrated as one of the nation's top soldiers since before the war began. The two men also had much in common. Both commanded the respect of their men, both had won a string of victories, and both were determined to do whatever it took to win the war. Tragically, "whatever it took" would mean the loss of tens of thousands of American lives each month.

As Grant led his troops down through Virginia toward Richmond, he and Lee faced off in a series of battles more deadly than any the nation had seen before. In the wooded area known as the Wilderness, bursts of gunpowder set the forest ablaze, causing men to burn up or choke to death as they fought. At the village of Spotsylvania, rows of soldiers charged into one another,

A New Birth of Freedom

When the Civil War began, Northerners fought to bring the South back into the Union. As the war went on, that cause became linked with another. On January 1, 1863, Lincoln's Emancipation Proclamation announced that slaves in the Confederacy were to be granted freedom. Later that year in his Gettysburg Address, Lincoln defined the war, and the nation itself, as being dedicated to the idea that all men are created equal.

Four score and seven years ago our fathers brought forth on this continent, a new nation, conceived in Liberty, and dedicated to the proposition that all men are created equal. Now we are engaged in a great civil war, testing whether that nation or any nation so conceived and so dedicated, can long endure.

Near the conclusion of his speech, Lincoln declared that "we here highly resolve that . . . this nation . . . shall have a new birth of freedom." From this point on the North fought not only to restore the Union but also to bring about a "new birth of freedom" by freeing the slaves.

hour after hour, until there were piles of corpses ten bodies deep. At a crossroads called Cold Harbor, Union soldiers pinned their names to their jackets so they could be easily identified if they were killed. They were wise to do so, for more than five thousand of these men were mowed down by Confederate bullets in half an hour.

In the North, people began calling Grant a butcher. He seemed willing to send young men to their death as though he didn't even care. But General Grant did care. Those closest to him could tell that the slaughter was causing him constant, quiet agony. He struggled to hide his feelings, smoking one cigar after another and whittling away at a piece of wood until there was nothing left. Alone in his tent after battle, he would cry aloud. As Horace Porter observed, "No one was more desirous of peace; no one was possessed of a heart more sensitive to every form of human suffering than the commander."

Unlike some other generals, Grant never enjoyed war for its own sake. He never found it beautiful or glorious. He believed the Union had to be saved, however, and slavery had to be ended. Grant believed that if the war were to be won, many people on both sides would have to die. He felt that as bad as things were on his side, it had to be even worse for the enemy.

He was right. The Confederates were running out of men. Their troops now included men in their sixties and boys in their early teens. Though General Lee's forces were outnumbered, they had the advantage of fighting on their own turf. They were fighting for their homeland, and Grant realized that defeating them would take patience.

But patience was in short supply in the North. As the presidential election of 1864 approached, Northerners were tired of the war and anxious for a new leader. The candidate running against Lincoln, George McClellan, was willing to make peace with the South by agreeing to let Southerners keep their slaves. If the Union army didn't have a breakthrough soon, McClellan would surely win the election and the cause of freedom for the slaves would be lost.

Then, in the nick of time, came good news for Grant and Lincoln: General Sherman had taken Atlanta. It became clear that Grant's overall strategy for defeating the South was working. People across the North celebrated the victory, regained their faith in the war, and reelected Lincoln. After a few more months of fighting, Grant sent Lee a note urging him to surrender. Southern defeat was so certain, Grant explained, that it was

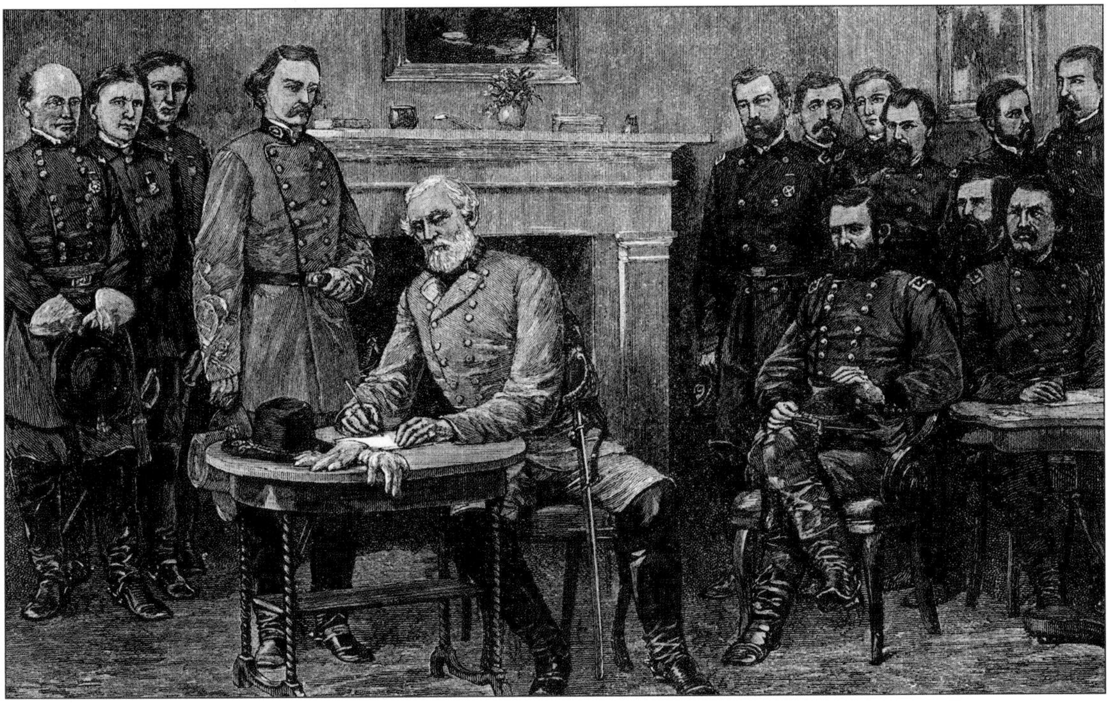

General Robert E. Lee signs a document of surrender at Appomattox, as General Grant looks on.

pointless for any more men to die. Eventually Lee came to realize Grant was right.

On April 9, 1865, at Appomattox Courthouse, Lee and Grant met to make the surrender official. Lee was dressed in a new uniform, with a red silk sash around his waist. His sword glittered, his boots were polished and shiny. Grant wore no special decorations and no sword, and his boots were spattered with mud. Grant's drab attire reflected his mood, since he was feeling little reason to celebrate. "My own feelings," Grant would later write, "were sad and depressed. I felt like anything rather than rejoicing at the downfall of a foe who had fought so long and valiantly, and had suffered so much for a cause—though that cause was, I believe, one of the worst for which a people ever fought."

In setting the terms of surrender, Grant proved extremely generous. He promised Lee that Confederate generals wouldn't be punished, and he allowed the defeated soldiers to lay down their arms and return home. He also let the men keep their horses, which they would need for farming. He offered to feed Lee's troops, who were on the verge of starvation. After leaving the courthouse, Grant refused to let his men celebrate victory. "The war is over," Grant announced to his troops. "The rebels are our countrymen again."

The Darkest Day

The next week Grant headed to Washington to meet with President Lincoln. Wherever the two men were seen together, people cheered. On the evening of April 14, Grant and his wife planned to join President and Mrs. Lincoln for an evening at the theater. At the last minute, though, Julia decided she and Ulysses should leave for New Jersey to see their children instead.

That decision disappointed an actor named John Wilkes Booth. A secessionist hungry for revenge, Booth had planned to steal into the theater during the show and shoot both Lincoln and Grant. Though Grant wasn't there when Booth sneaked into the theater, Lincoln was.

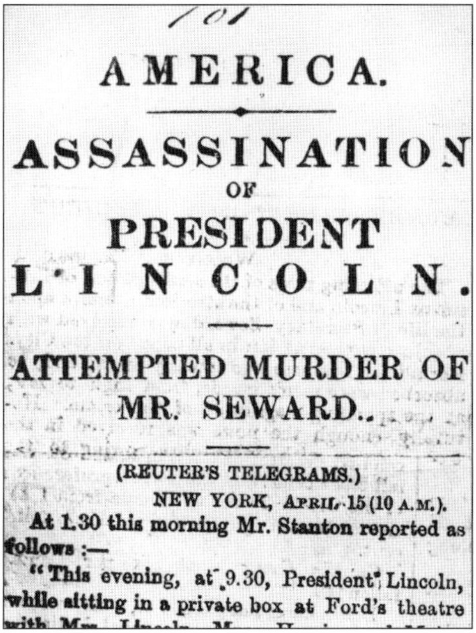

AMERICA.

ASSASSINATION OF PRESIDENT LINCOLN.

ATTEMPTED MURDER OF MR. SEWARD.

(REUTER'S TELEGRAMS.)

NEW YORK, APRIL 15 (10 A.M.).

At 1.30 this morning Mr. Stanton reported as follows :—

"This evening, at 9.30, President Lincoln, while sitting in a private box at Ford's theatre

On April 15, 1865, the report of President Lincoln's assassination hit the news.

"It was the darkest day of my life," Grant said when he heard that the president had been assassinated. For years Grant felt guilty for not having been at the theater that night. If he had been there, Grant believed, he might have saved the admired leader who had become his friend. Historian Geoffrey Perret wrote:

> *Grant was certain that he would have heard Booth open the door to Lincoln's box and been able to get his body between Booth's derringer and the seated President. His admiration for Lincoln added to the sense of loss and kept alive that feeling of guilt.*

Still grieving, Grant returned to Washington to serve under the new president, Andrew Johnson.

Johnson and Reconstruction

Johnson, a Unionist from Tennessee, had been the only southern senator to stay with the Union when the Civil War broke out.

When Lincoln ran for president in 1864, Republicans chose Johnson as Lincoln's running mate to try to reach out to the South. Though Lincoln got the country through the Civil War, Johnson would have to face the extremely difficult postwar challenge called **Reconstruction**.

There were many different ideas for how the South should be "reconstructed," or brought back into the Union. Some people thought former rebels should simply be forgiven and made citizens again. Others felt they should be punished for revolting against the U.S. government. There was also the question of how to deal with the "**freedmen**," the former slaves who made up nearly half of the South's population. Some reasoned they should be given all the rights of citizenship at once, including the right to vote. Others thought they should be given those rights gradually. Still others argued they should never be given equal rights.

Any plan for Reconstruction would have to begin with Union troops keeping order in the South. So as President Johnson tried to carry out his plans for Reconstruction, he needed the support of the nation's top general. He didn't always get it. When Johnson tried to have Confederate generals put on trial for **treason**—a crime punishable by death, Grant said that would break the promise he had made to Lee at Appomattox, and he threatened to resign. Johnson backed down.

This was only the first of many disagreements Johnson and Grant were to have about Reconstruction. In May 1866 wild mobs of whites charged through African-American neighborhoods in Memphis, Tennessee, burning buildings and killing dozens of people. Local officials did nothing to stop the rioting. In fact, many of the rioters were off-duty policemen. After the army had restored order, Grant wanted to use the army to make sure the troublemakers were punished. Johnson wouldn't let him. Grant was furious at the way white Southerners were becoming rebellious again. He told a *New York Times* reporter, "A year ago they were willing to do anything; now they regard themselves as masters of the situation."

The following summer there were more riots in other southern towns and more murders. Southern whites were becoming defiant, and the president didn't seem to mind. "This country is for white men," President Johnson said. To make sure that the country remained ruled by white men, Johnson allowed southern state governments to maintain Black Codes that limited the rights of African Americans. Under these codes, black citizens could be forced to work in certain jobs, for certain bosses, for little or no pay. If they displeased their bosses in any way, they could be thrown in jail. Grant began to feel that if Johnson had his way, the cause of freedom for which he had fought the Civil War would be lost.

Many Republicans in Congress were totally opposed to Johnson's plan for Reconstruction. Radicals, as they were called, were determined to make the freedmen full citizens right away. As the **Radical Republicans** passed laws to give freedmen more power, President Johnson battled them at every step. Finally leaders in Congress decided to **impeach** Johnson—to put him on trial in an attempt to remove him from office.

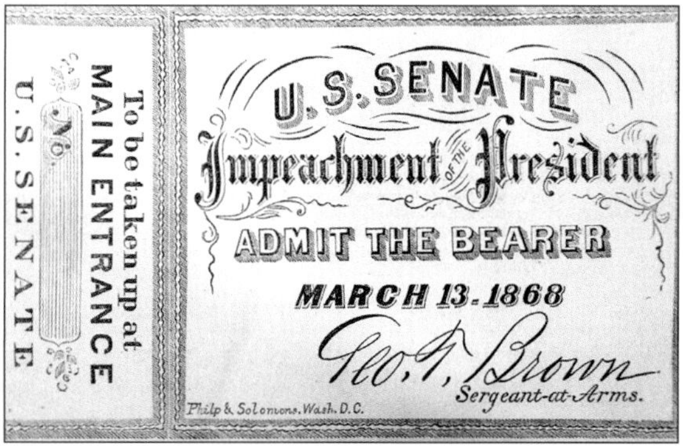

Thousands of tickets were printed for the admission to the impeachment trial of President Andrew Johnson.

Though Johnson's opponents fell one short in their effort to remove him from office, his reputation as a leader was damaged. As the election of 1868 approached, Americans wanted a new president who would get along better with Congress.

The Election of 1868

When Republicans met at their national convention to select their candidate, they voted unanimously for Ulysses Grant. No one was sure exactly what Grant's views were on Reconstruction, or on other issues. Most people assumed he was moderate, without strong political views, and they liked that. At that explosive time, he was the one leader whom hardly anybody hated. Grant was

On May 21, 1868, the Republican National Convention in Chicago nominated Grant for president and Schuyler Colfax of Indiana for vice president.

loved throughout the North for his leadership skills, and admired in the South for the mercy he had shown the defeated troops. To Republicans it seemed that if anyone could bring people together, it was Grant.

Upon hearing the news that he was nominated for president, Grant showed no emotion. He probably wasn't surprised. For years people had been suggesting that he run for president. Now he seemed to sense the time was right. In his letter accepting the nomination, Grant closed with a simple phrase that was exactly what people, North and South, wanted to hear: "Let us have peace."

In those days most candidates would choose to sit out campaigns, letting members of their parties do the legwork. Grant had no interest in public speaking, so he was glad to remain silent. But his supporters were aggressive and loud. They called Democratic candidate Horatio Seymour a traitor to the Union, and claimed that Democrats were rebels in disguise. Democrats in turn labelled Grant a drunk and accused Republicans of trying to "Africanize" the South.

After voting, Grant spent election day at the house of a friend, Illinois congressman Elihu Washburne. Washburne had had a telegraph line installed so they could follow the news as the votes were counted. As the results came in, it became clear that the vote would be close. Near dawn Grant walked home to find Julia waiting for him on the front step. "I am afraid," he informed her, "that I am elected."

PRESIDENT GRANT *Five*

When Grant took office, the nation was swept by a wave of good feeling. The new president was young—at forty-six he was the youngest president yet. He was new to politics, so he had no political favors to repay or enemies in Congress. In his brief inauguration speech Grant dealt with controversial issues like Reconstruction as delicately as possible:

> *The country having just emerged from a great rebellion, many questions will come before it in the next four years which preceding administrations have never had to deal with. In meeting these it is desirable that they should be approached calmly, without prejudice, hate, or sectional pride, remembering that the greatest good to the greatest number is the object to be required.*

He spent more time talking about the economy and the need to pay off money the government had borrowed during the Civil War. He finished by urging the different sections of the country to show patience and understanding toward one another.

Though Grant's speech pleased the public, his first act as president threw Congress into an uproar. In choosing his cabinet, Grant selected friends and army officers but not one politician who was popular with Congress. Some of the men Grant chose proved to be unqualified for their jobs. Some others proved to be excellent. But by making his choices without consulting leaders in Congress, Grant had upset powerful men whose support he would need.

President Grant, seated with his Cabinet, found working with politicians very different from working with soldiers.

In this single step Grant exposed a problem that would haunt him throughout his presidency. As a general, he had succeeded by ignoring the old rules and doing things his own way. As president, however, that wouldn't work. Politics involves compromise and making deals. Grant had little patience for this sort of give and take.

Grant and Reconstruction

Grant got along just fine with Congress, though, in the way he handled Reconstruction. He pardoned leaders of the Confederacy for their roles in the war. He sent troops to the South to support Radical Reconstruction. And he supported the Fifteenth Amendment to the **Constitution**, which granted freedmen the right to vote.

Grant thought that when freedmen could vote, they would be able to protect their rights themselves and troops would no longer be needed. But no one in the North imagined the fury that would erupt in the South when freed slaves began voting. To take power back from freedmen, some Southern whites joined secret terrorist organizations. In the largest of these, the Ku Klux Klan, members would put on bedsheets to pose as the ghosts of Confederate soldiers. After dark, mobs of these hooded terrorists would break into the homes of African Americans who had voted or stood up for their rights in any way, and also into the homes of whites who had supported blacks. Then they would beat up, burn, hang, or cut up their

Inaugural Absences

According to tradition, when a new president is sworn in on Inauguration Day, the outgoing president is on hand. This shows the world that the transfer of power is peaceful and happy. But when Grant became president, Andrew Johnson was feeling anything but happy. His disagreements with Grant about Reconstruction had left both men bitter. When Grant's carriage stopped at the White House on the way to the Capitol Building, Johnson said he was too busy to come.

In 1801 President John Adams had avoided the inauguration of his successor, Thomas Jefferson. And in 1829 Adams's son, President John Quincy Adams, had sidestepped the inauguration of his successor, Andrew Jackson. Grant's inauguration was the third and last time a departing president was absent as the new president was sworn in.

Known for terrorizing blacks, members of the Ku Klux Klan called their organization the Invisible Empire of the South.

victims, often with the victims' loved ones looking on. This brutality was meant to inflict pain on those who died and to terrify those who lived.

Grant wouldn't stand for it. Acting more like a general than a president, he ordered the military into the South to round up members of the organization. Then he asked Congress to pass laws that would allow the federal government to punish the terrorists. Congress hesitated. Local governments, not the federal government, were supposed to see that people were tried for crimes committed in their **jurisdictions**. But Grant pointed out that white Southern leaders would never punish the Ku Klux Klan, since many of them supported the Klan. As Grant saw it, if the federal government didn't stand up to the Klan, no one would.

In response to Grant's demand, Congress passed the Ku Klux Klan Act, which allowed the federal government to punish

Without Distinction to Race

Even when race relations were at their worst, not all Southern whites were racist. Some even dared to break with their neighbors and support Reconstruction. In a letter to the Reconstruction governor of South Carolina, one Southern white man wrote:

I am a poor man . . . hated for nothing else but my loyalty to the mother government. . . . But I rejoice to think that God almighty has given the poor of South Carolina a Governor to protect the humble poor without distinction to race or color.

the terrorists. Across the South thousands of Klan members were tried and put in jail. Decades later another version of the Ku Klux Klan would rise up, but for the time being, the Ku Klux Klan was dead.

With terrorism under control, African Americans were able to vote and to hold office. Many were elected to serve in local and state governments. A few were even elected to serve in the United States Congress. Some Southern whites complained that Reconstruction gave blacks too much power. Although 45 percent of the South's population was African American, the percentage of African-American leaders under Reconstruction was rarely that high. Under Grant the South saw the fairest elections it would have until the 1960s.

Native-American Issues

Another race of Americans that Grant sought to protect was a group of people who had not been regarded as American—or even as people—the Native Americans. Ever since the first European settlers had come to America, white men had been pushing Native Americans out of their lands. As the United States expanded, its leaders made promises to push the Native Americans only so far and no farther. Each of these promises was broken. Not surprisingly, some Native Americans responded by attacking settlers. When generals of the United States Army were ordered to "keep the peace," they commonly would try to wipe out entire Native-American tribes. General Philip Sheridan's claim that "the only good Indian is a dead Indian" was typical of how these military men felt.

In the election of 1868, many Westerners voted for Grant, hoping he would prove to be this sort of military man. But instead of attacking Native Americans, Grant put forth a peace policy to protect them. As part of this policy, Quakers and other religious groups would work with Native Americans to set up communities, schools, and churches. Grant believed that if Native Americans would give up their "primitive" ways and become "civilized," the fighting between them and the whites would end. Today we realize that this approach was simpleminded and disrespectful of Native-American culture. But for its time, Grant's peace policy may be seen as a step forward. The idea that Native Americans should be treated as human beings with rights and dignity was something few U.S. citizens had even considered.

FOREIGN AFFAIRS

In foreign affairs Grant also proved to be a man of peace. As Mexico struggled to defend itself against European powers Grant began to feel that the United States needed territory near South America that could be used to defend the U.S. mainland. Unlike previous presidents, Grant had no interest in gaining land by force. So when the leader of Santo Domingo, the Caribbean island now known as the Dominican Republic, offered to sell the United States the right to "**annex**," or add on, his island country, Grant was interested. At once Grant sent his aide, Orville Babcock, to visit Santo Domingo to see what it was like. Babcock returned with samples of precious minerals he had found in the soil—and a signed treaty. Knowing how anxious Grant was to add Santo Domingo to the United States, Babcock had gone ahead and made the deal on his own.

Grant quickly realized that the treaty was meaningless. Treaties are made by a nation's top leaders, not by their assistants. Grant was so excited about the deal, however, that he asked Congress to approve it anyway. As the members of Congress debated, they came up with many reasons for not wanting to annex Santo Domingo. But the real reason they rejected the idea was that they just didn't like Grant's way of doing things. He had ignored the rules, stepped on their toes, and had to be punished. Grant never forgave Congress for refusing what he felt was a fine opportunity. A few decades later the United States acquired Puerto Rico and the United States Virgin Islands as the spoils of battle and bullying. Grant's plan for gaining territory in the Caribbean had been peaceful.

After failing with his Santo Domingo efforts, Grant had a major foreign policy success that involved Great Britain. During the Civil War the British had sold the South a cruiser, the *Alabama*, which the Confederates had used to sink or steal over sixty Union ships. After the war many Americans wanted revenge on the British for the damage done by the *Alabama*. Members of Congress suggested that the United States seize Canada, which was then owned by Britain, as repayment. Some were calling for war with Britain.

Grant understood the nation's anger. But he didn't want to go to war. Instead, he agreed to resolve the dispute in a new way: by letting an international panel decide. Representatives from the United States, Britain, Switzerland, Italy, and Brazil met in Geneva, Switzerland, to come up with a solution. After considering both sides of the argument, the panel agreed that Great Britain should pay the United States $15.5 million. American anger was calmed. British pride was preserved. War was avoided. And, most importantly, leaders around the world had witnessed a new way nations could solve their differences without killing people.

At Home in the White House

By the time Grant's term was drawing to a close, the president had settled into a comfortable routine. Each morning he would wake at seven o'clock, read the paper, have breakfast at eight-thirty, and get to the office by ten o'clock. After work he'd unwind by taking a ride in a carriage drawn by Thoroughbred horses. Once he got so carried away with the joy of a carriage outing that he was stopped by the police for speeding. Sometimes, instead of riding, he'd go for a walk, stopping to join boys in the park playing the new game called baseball.

Throughout his years in office, the young president was a devoted family man. Though his oldest sons were away at college, Nellie and Jesse grew up in the White House, where Grant had a playroom built just for them. Grant always found time to see the children at meals, on weekends, and during their frequent family vacations at the New Jersey shore.

He made even more time for Julia. The president and his wife walked everywhere arm in arm, or holding hands, and would often pass notes during the day. When she first came to the White House, Julia wanted to have an operation on her eye so the country wouldn't have a First Lady who was cross-eyed. But Grant told Julia she looked beautiful as she was and insisted she stay that way, and so she did. With her lively personality, Julia was the perfect hostess for White House parties. A popular First Lady, she found living in the White House "a bright and beautiful dream."

Reelection

As the election of 1872 approached, a group of Republicans who opposed Radical Reconstruction and didn't like Grant broke away from the party. Calling themselves **Liberal Republicans**, they chose New York newspaper publisher Horace Greeley to run against Grant. **Democrats** made Greeley their candidate, too, and teamed up with the Liberal Republicans to prevent Grant from being reelected.

Even with these two parties working to beat him, Grant won the election by a huge margin. He believed this meant that the American people were happy with his work, and that pleased him. The presidency hadn't been a smooth ride for Grant. At times it had been extremely bumpy. Somehow, for the most part, though, he had stayed in control and kept the country moving forward. Shortly, that would change.

A former supporter of Grant, Horace Greeley joined the Liberal Republicans and ran for president against him, winning only 43 percent of the vote.

The Second Term

Six

When Grant was on the battlefield, he was always able to think quickly and adjust if the situation suddenly changed. During his second term as president, however, Grant was presented with a new situation to which he could never adequately adjust. This situation, in which Grant and everyone else in the country found themselves, is called the Gilded Age. Historians refer to the last part of the nineteenth century as gilded (meaning "covered in gold") because it was known for metal, money, and greed. After the Civil War the country saw the birth of huge corporations that built and ran railroads, iron and steel factories, and telegraph services. The owners of these corporations became incredibly rich. People who bought **stock** in the corporations could become rich, too. But while some people made money quickly, others lost money even more quickly. These unfortunate souls, whose lack of experience in the ways of wealth made them easily tricked, were called suckers.

Once the newly rich realized they could protect their wealth by working with politicians, politics was never the same. Before the Civil War politics had been about such ideas as slavery and **states' rights**. In the Gilded Age politics was about money. Greed infected local governments in the North and South alike and swept through the federal government like a plague. Although Grant was never good at business, he had always admired those who were. This made him the perfect sucker. Early in his first term Grant's friendships with tricky businessmen had caused him some embarrassment. In his second term such friendships would cost him even more dearly.

The Gilded Age was a time in U.S. history when some Americans achieved incredible wealth.

Scandal and Panic

During Grant's reelection campaign a scandal exploded into public view. The main scoundrels involved were the owners of Union Pacific Railroad, who were receiving government money to build tracks across the country. These railroad men found they could keep some of the government money for themselves if they pretended to be paying it to a made-up company. That company was called Crédit Mobilier. To keep the government from interfering with this scam, the owners bribed many members of Congress.

Grant's vice president, Schulyer Colfax, was found to have been bribed by Union Pacific, too, so Grant replaced him with Massachusetts Senator Henry Wilson—who also turned out to have been bribed by Union Pacific! Though Grant himself was never found to have been bribed, the Crédit Mobilier scandal filled Americans with a general distrust of their government.

Their distrust turned to disgust when the nation was hit by the Panic of 1873. Until then, Americans had complete confidence in the success of the railroad companies. As with the Internet companies that had such success in the late twentieth century, people believed the railroads would keep getting bigger, better, and richer. But in September 1873 the stock price of Northern Pacific Railway suddenly plunged. There were so few big companies in those days that the failure of just one of them could upset the entire economy. At once there was widespread panic. Banks closed. Factories closed. Small farmers, who depended on trains to move their crops, were hurt worst of all.

In September 1873, many banks and businesses closed, causing widespread panic.

To provide quick relief, Congress passed a

bill ordering $100 million in new paper money to be printed. They sent the bill to the president for him to sign it into law. Grant remembered the pain of being poor, so he decided to sign the bill—and then changed his mind. He believed the new paper money would cause **inflation**, and lead foreign countries to lose respect for the American dollar. In Grant's eyes the bill would help the poor in the short run but hurt the whole country in the long run. So he didn't sign it, and the new money wasn't printed.

Grant realized that not signing this popular bill would hurt his party in the coming Congressional elections, and it did. In the midterm elections of 1874, the Democrats won control of Congress for the first time since 1860, with a comfortable majority of sixty votes. His party's loss of Congress wasn't entirely Grant's fault, though. In hard times voters become less idealistic. Northern whites were losing interest in the rights of Southern blacks, and turning away from the Republican Party which had stood up for equal rights for freedmen. They began to support the Democratic Party, which believed the federal government should leave the South alone.

Meanwhile, the laws Grant and the Republicans had passed to protect African Americans were being stripped away. The Supreme Court found the Ku Klux Klan Act unconstitutional, and threw it out. The federal government would no longer be able to put offenders on trial for acts of terrorism aimed at African Americans. A **civil rights** law Grant had promised to deliver also ran into trouble. That law would have guaranteed African Americans the right to go to public schools and to be treated as the equals of whites in all public places, but the law was watered down in the Democratic Congress. Even after being passed in its milder form, it was eventually thrown out by the Supreme Court.

Corruption

In an effort to further weaken Grant, Democrats in Congress began to investigate his administration for corruption. When they did, a staggering number of the people with whom Grant

The Supremely Conservative Court

By the middle of his second term Grant had appointed four of the justices on the Supreme Court. Even so, some of Grant's own court appointees voted to overturn laws that Grant relied on to protect the rights of African Americans. This marked the beginning of a conservative period in which the federal government would be barred from playing a role in African Americans' struggle for civil rights. Charles Warren, a legal scholar, summarized the reasoning of these conservative justices:

There can be no question that the decisions in these cases were most fortunate. They largely eliminated from national politics the negro question which had so long embittered congressional debates; they relegated the burden and duty of protecting the negro to the states, to whom they properly belonged, and they served to restore confidence in the national court in the southern states.

Justice Ward Hunt, the lone dissenter in one of the cases, noted that the court had brought to "an impotent conclusion the vigorous Amendments on the subject of slavery." It was not until the 1950s that the Supreme Court, under Chief Justice Earl Warren, would become once again "vigorous" in protecting the rights of African Americans.

had surrounded himself were found to be steeped in Gilded Age corruption. The minister (as American ambassadors were then called) to England was selling stock in a mine that didn't exist. The minister to Brazil had pressured the Brazilian government to pay him $100,000 for a false claim. The attorney general had used government money to buy himself a fancy carriage and to keep well-dressed servants. The navy secretary was taking bribes in return for allowing ships to be poorly built. The treasury secretary was letting a tax collector keep half of the money he collected. The secretary of war was taking bribes to let certain companies sell their goods on reservations where Native Americans lived.

The illegal operation that came closest to Grant himself, however, was the Whiskey Ring. For years distillers in Missouri had avoided paying tax on the whiskey they sold by bribing federal agents. In this way they had been robbing the taxpayers of millions of dollars a year. When Grant learned about the crime, he told investigators, "Let no guilty man escape." Unfortunately for

This political cartoon satirizes Grant's strenuous efforts to keep his scandal-rocked administration from falling apart.

Grant, the investigators came to believe that one of the guilty men was Grant's aide Orville Babcock. Apparently Babcock had used Whiskey Ring money to help pay for Grant's reelection campaign. Grant testified on behalf of his trusted aide, so Babcock wasn't found guilty in court. But 110 others were.

Even in today's age of corruption and greed, it's hard to imagine how Grant could have let himself become so completely surrounded by criminals. In commanding soldiers his ability to keep his men in line was remarkable. In facing enemies his ability to predict human behavior had been impressive. In appointing generals his judgment had been superb. But in politics he was often a poor judge of character. Grant himself was never found to be dishonest in any way. But each time another member of his staff was charged with a crime it caused Grant more embarrassment, and made it harder for him to focus on other issues. And the loss of focus for Grant meant a loss of freedom for millions of African Americans in the South.

Retreat from Reconstruction

While the president was busy dealing with his staff's corruption, Southern whites were able to "redeem," or take back, their state governments, one state at a time. In Louisiana the redemption movement was led by an army called the White Leaguers. Unlike the secretive Ku Klux Klan, whose members worked in darkness, the White Leaguers would march in broad daylight. Unmasked and unashamed, they disrupted government meetings, physically removed elected leaders from their seats, and replaced them with men of their own choosing.

In response to the White Leaguers, Grant sent five thousand troops to Louisiana to see that the elected officials were put back in their seats. But Grant's use of force caused an uproar, and not only in the South. Even in New England, where slavery had been most despised, citizens now came together to express their fury at what Grant had done. The image of the United States Army marching into the Louisiana statehouse with raised bayonets made people feel that the federal government had gone too far.

A few months later, as the election of 1875 approached, the governor of Mississippi asked Grant for help. White militias were threatening to disrupt the election and throw out the Republican government. Grant wanted to avoid sending in the army at all costs, so he made a deal with the leaders of the militias: he agreed not to send in troops in return for the militias' promise to lay down their arms.

But, on the night before the election, the promise was broken. Armed whites drove African Americans from their homes and threatened to kill them if they tried to vote. On the day of elections Democrats destroyed **ballot** boxes where African Americans had voted, or just replaced Republican votes with their own. Not surprisingly, Democrats won almost every seat in Mississippi. The few Republicans who were elected that day were either chased from town or assassinated.

Until the end of this bloody struggle, the governor of Mississippi begged Grant to send troops. But Grant believed the presence of troops would only stir up more anger and cost Republicans votes in the North, so he did nothing. Grant would never retrace his steps, and as a general he never surrendered, as president he felt forced to retreat. Many Republicans wanted Grant to run for a third term. So did the First Lady, Julia. But Grant had had enough.

The next year, in a wave of anti-Reconstruction feeling, the Democrats won the **popular vote** for the first time since the Civil War. When the **electoral votes** were disputed, Democrats agreed to accept Republican Rutherford B. Hayes as the winner, on the condition that he promised to end Reconstruction. So when Grant left the White House, the last federal troops left the South, along with any hope that freedmen would be treated as citizens. The "new birth of freedom" that Lincoln promised and Grant tried to achieve would have to wait for nearly a hundred years.

Out of Power

Seven

On leaving the White House, Grant said he felt as excited as a boy out of school. So he decided to do what boys just out of school often do—he took a vacation. On May 17, 1877, with family and friends, former president Grant boarded a ship and set out to see the world.

Around the World

Though Grant's policies had made him unpopular in parts of the United States, overseas he was treated like a superstar. As historian Jean Edward Smith described it, "To heads of state and the public alike he was the most famous soldier of the era, personifying the marvel of a modern industrial power." Queen Victoria of England, Czar Alexander of Russia, Chancellor Bismarck of Germany, and Pope Leo XIII were among the dozens of world leaders who met with the "Hero of Appomattox," entertained him, and asked his advice. Grant was even more adored by the working people he met on his travels. They saw Grant as a common man who had risen to power to defend the powerless.

Though his royal hosts were anxious to show him military parades, Grant avoided these whenever possible. He had seen enough armies at home. Instead, he preferred taking in natural wonders, famous buildings, and museums. He spent days admiring the paintings in the Louvre Museum in Paris, visited the Sistine Chapel in Rome, toured the ancient pyramids in Egypt, and the biblical landmarks in the Holy Land. In Turkey, Sultan Abdul Hamid II offered to let Grant have any two of his splendid

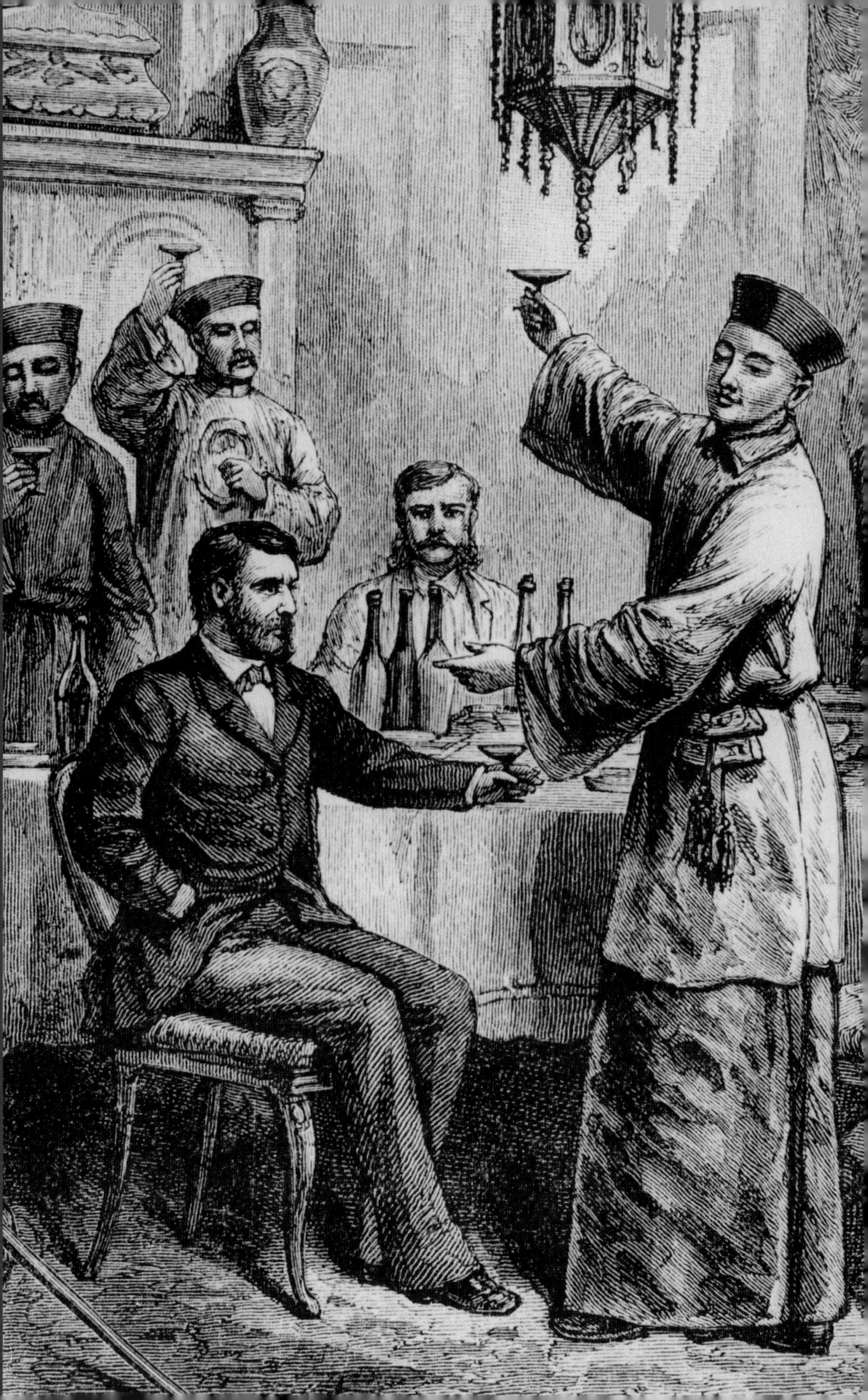

After leaving the presidency, Grant visited many parts of the world, including the Near East.

Arabian stallions. Grant spent a few hours carefully picking out his favorites.

After traveling all through Europe and the Middle East, Grant progressed to the Far East. He toured India, Siam (now Thailand), Hong Kong, and China—which Grant predicted would one day rise to become a world power. Then it was on to Japan, where Grant was honored with fireworks, cheering crowds waving American flags, and several meetings with the emperor of Japan. From there Grant wanted to press on to Australia, but Julia felt it was time to head home. After all, they had been traveling for over two years.

The Election of 1880

When Grant returned to the United States, the presidential election of 1880 was approaching and the Republican Party needed a candidate. No president had ever been elected to a third term. But Grant's followers were passionate and persistent, and Grant himself felt refreshed by travel. So when it was time for the Republican convention, Grant let his supporters try to nominate him for yet another term.

On the first ballot Grant had more votes than any other candidate but not quite the majority needed for nomination. On the second ballot Grant once again led the voting but still lacked a majority. On ballot after ballot Grant's supporters stood firm. After two days of voting, though, momentum shifted to Congressman James A. Garfield, who went on to win the Republican nomination and the presidency.

A Double Dose of Tragedy

Nowadays retired presidents get a **pension** that provides a steady income. But in Grant's day former presidents had to look for work just like anyone else. So when Grant's son Buck (as Ulysses Junior was called) approached him with a business plan, Grant was interested. Buck had formed an investment firm called Grant and Ward with his friend Ferdinand Ward, who was thought to have a gift for making shrewd investments. Buck and his friend invited the retired president to join the company as a "silent partner," which meant Grant would provide money and Ward would manage it.

For a few years the company seemed to be doing well. Grant believed he was quietly getting rich. Then, in early 1884, Ward came to Grant with a desperate request. The company needed quick cash, Ward explained, and a lot of it, to get through a difficult period. During the Panic of 1873 President Grant had been cautious and strict in handling the nation's money. But when it came to handling his own money, he was just as naive as he had been as a boy. Shortly after Grant gave Ward the enormous sum he had asked for, Grant and Ward went out of business, and Ward, who had been secretly lying and stealing for years, was arrested and jailed. Besides breaking the law, Ward had broken Grant's heart. "I don't see how I can ever trust any human being again," he said. At this point, Grant had only $80 left. Julia had $130.

It was hard to imagine that things could get worse for Grant, but they did. One day while eating a peach, he jumped up from the table in pain. His throat felt as if it were on fire. Though he tried to ignore the pain, it wouldn't go away. Eventually Grant learned the devastating truth from a doctor: he had throat cancer. As the cancer got worse, Grant realized that he might soon be leaving Julia a penniless widow. At once he came up with a plan.

The Final Battle

For some time publishers had been asking Grant to write his Civil War memoirs. Grant never thought of himself as a writer, so he refused their offers. Now, to provide for Julia, Grant decided to tell his story after all. If Grant had signed with the wrong publisher he might once again have been swindled. But, luckily, the famous writer Mark Twain, who had become a friend of Grant's, offered to publish the book and give Grant a generous 70 percent of the profits.

So Grant got to work. For weeks, and then months, he wrote. What began as a chore became an obsession. As he worked to get every detail right, the battles at Donelson, Shiloh, Vicksburg, and Cold Harbor came alive once again in his mind. At first Grant worked by dictating to a secretary, Noble Dawson. "As he went on his voice became weaker and weaker," Dawson would later recall. "And toward the last, I had to take my seat very close to his, and he whispered his words in my ear while I took them down in shorthand." At the point when even whispering became too painful, Grant wrote out the book himself.

Grant writes his memoirs on the front porch of his cottage in Mount McGregor.

That summer the growth in Grant's throat became so

large he couldn't lie down for fear of choking, so he slept sitting up. As the pain of swallowing became unbearable, he lost interest in eating and lost 50 pounds. He grew so weak he could hardly walk. His writing became blurred and scratchy. "He was very weak," Dawson remembered, "and his hand grew more and more trembling." Yet Grant continued. Relatives were afraid writing was killing him. But his doctor felt that it was keeping him alive. In spite of the terrible pain, Grant was going to finish this book. It was his last battle, and there would be no retreat.

When the news spread that Grant was dying, visitors from across the country came to the cottage where he was staying, at Mount McGregor, in upstate New York. As Grant sat on his porch wrapped in blankets, thousands of Union veterans filed past to get a last look at their hero. His friends from war and

Grant (center) poses with his family at Mount McGregor shortly before his death.

Happy Ending

In writing his memoirs Grant hadn't had time to cover his presidency in detail. But he did manage to provide an in-depth account of his Civil War experiences, and to offer thoughts about the future in closing. In the final paragraphs of the conclusion, Grant wrote:

I feel that we are on the eve of a new era, when there is to be great harmony between the Federal and Confederate. I cannot stay to be a living witness to the correctness of this prophecy; but I feel it within me that it is to be so. The universally kind feeling expressed for me at a time when it was supposed that each day would prove my last, seemed to me the beginning of the answer to "Let us have peace."

Though in tremendous pain at the time, Grant managed to finish with a passage that is optimistic and uplifting.

politics came to visit, too. Grant's longest visit was with his old friend Simon Bolivar Buckner, from whom Grant had demanded unconditional surrender at Donelson. Buckner told Grant how grateful Southerners were for the kind terms Grant offered at Appomattox, and thanked him for sticking up for Southern officers when Andrew Johnson wanted to put them on trial. Unable to speak, Grant wrote Buckner a note saying, "I have witnessed since my sickness just what I wished to see ever since the war: harmony and good feeling between the sections."

On July 16, 1885, Grant finished his memoirs. In less than a year he had written a book of over 1,200 pages. A few days later

Grant asked to be moved to the bed, where Julia sat up with him through the night holding his hand. On the morning of July 23, Grant quietly died. He was sixty-three years old. In his robe was a note he had written saying good-bye to Julia and a locket with a strand of her hair.

Before Grant's death Mark Twain had told him that there were over 100,000 advance orders for his memoirs, titled

Final Resting Place

The Gilded Age wasn't known for restraint. And when the great American hero of the age died, his fans spared no expense. In the biggest fund-raising campaign yet waged, the eighteenth president's supporters raised $600,000 and built him the largest tomb on the continent of North America. Etched in its marble and granite walls are mosaic murals showing Grant at Vicksburg and Appomattox, and his famous words "Let Us Have Peace." In this elegant structure overlooking New York City's Hudson River, Ulysses and Julia Grant rest in peace, undisturbed by their 100,000 annual visitors.

Personal Memoirs of Ulysses S. Grant. So Grant died knowing his book would make money. But he could never have imagined it would be so highly praised. Many intellectuals had regarded Grant as a great warrior but not much of a thinker—until they read his book. On page after page Grant describes the war with such clarity and care that a reader can grasp the complexities of each battle and feel the drama as it unfolds. Novelist and playwright Gertrude Stein pronounced it one of the greatest books ever written by an American. Literary critic Edmund Wilson called it "a unique expression of national character." And Twain called it the greatest war memoir since Julius Caesar's, written two thousand years earlier. Eventually more than 300,000 copies of Grant's memoirs were sold. They earned nearly half a million dollars for Julia. In his hard-fought, final battle Grant was victorious.

Looking Back at Grant

In the years after Grant's death, many people began to view his presidency as a failure. One reason for this is the scandals that surrounded his administration. Another reason is Grant's own modesty. Historians were quick to quote Grant's private remarks that he should never have been president, though they ignored his similar statements about his military service and his writing.

A third reason for Grant's unpopularity has to do with the peculiar nature of the Civil War. After a war the winners usually write the history books. After the Civil War, though, Northerners were so eager to welcome the South back into the Union that they allowed the story of the war to be told from a Southern viewpoint. Three aspects of this point of view are that the war was about states' rights, not about slavery; that the North won because it had more troops, though Southern troops fought more bravely; and that Radical Reconstruction was an attempt by Northern politicians to rob and humiliate the South. These ideas were put forth in some history books, and in several movies and television programs as well. As a number of Americans began to see the Southern cause as noble and Reconstruction as mean-spirited, they lost some respect for the man who defeated the South, ended the war, and enforced Reconstruction.

But since the 1960s, historians have come to see Grant in a different light. Most agree that as a general he fought to keep the Union together and to free the slaves. Then as president he tried to see to it that when the South was restored to the Union, African Americans would become full citizens. Though his efforts to accomplish this caused intense anger and were eventually defeated, he made progress, however briefly, toward a great goal.

The issues left unfinished by the Civil War continue to cause division and pain long after Grant's presidency. But only two weeks after his death the nation enjoyed a moment of true unity. At Grant's funeral procession in New York City, 1.5 million people came out to see the coffin carrying his body being wheeled slowly up Broadway toward his tomb in Riverside Park. Although Julia, still grief stricken, wasn't there, President Grover Cleveland and two former presidents were there to honor him. As Grant had requested, soldiers from both sides of the Civil War marched alongside his coffin. So Sherman marched with Buckner, Union veterans marched with Confederates, and African American soldiers marched with whites. It was an event Grant would have loved: 60,000 Americans, Northern and Southern, black and white, all moving along, to the same beat, together.

Ulysses S. Grant, eighteenth president of the United States tried to heal divisions in nation and to obtain rights for African Americans.

Timeline

April 27, 1822
Born in Point Pleasant, Ohio

1843
Graduates from the United States Military Academy at West Point

1845
Fights in the Mexican War

1848
Marries Julia Dent

1854
Leaves the army

1862
In command of battle at Shiloh; appointed major general

1861
Rejoins the army

1863
Wins victory at Vicksburg

1864
Appointed lieutenant general

1820

1865
Receives Lee's surrender at Appomattox. Abraham Lincoln assassinated.

1866
Appointed general of the army

1868
Elected president

1872
Reelected president

1877
Starts worldwide travels

1880
Defeated for Republican nomination

July 16, 1885 Completes memoirs

July 23, 1885
Dies at Mount McGregor, New York

1890

Glossary

annex to add a smaller country or state on to a larger one

ballot a sheet of paper on which a vote is cast; or a round of voting

civil rights privileges to which citizens are entitled

Confederacy the eleven southern states that seceded from the United States marking the onset of the American Civil War

Constitution The document that outlines the basic laws by which the United States government operates

Democrat one of America's two major political parties, founded in 1828

depression a period in which an economy suffers, usually involving unemployment, falling prices, and failing businesses

electoral vote votes cast during national presidential elections by specially chosen representatives from each state

freedmen people who have been freed from slavery

impeach to formally charge an official with a crime in an attempt to remove him or her from office

inauguration a formal ceremony marking the beginning of a leader's term

inflation an increase in prices and/or a decrease in the value of money

jurisdiction a territorial range of control

Liberal Republicans a group of Republicans who broke away from their party in 1872 to oppose the reelection of President Grant

manifest destiny the concept, popular during the mid-1800s, that the United States had the moral right to expand westward to the Pacific Ocean

pension a sum of money paid regularly upon retirement

popular vote votes cast by citizens

quartermaster an army officer in charge of providing a group of troops with clothing and supplies

Radical Republicans members of the Republican Party who were most strongly opposed to slavery

Reconstruction the process of bringing the states of the former Confederacy back into the Union

Republican Party one of America's two major political parties, founded in 1854

secede to break away from a membership or alliance

secessionists people who believed southern states had a right to leave the Union

states' rights the right of states to govern their own affairs without the interference of the federal government

stock the ownership element of a corporation that is divided to give owners interest and voting rights

supply line a route by which such vital goods as food and weapons can be trasported to an army

treason an act by which someone betrays his or her country

unconditional surrender an act of surrender which is total and complete, without any deal making or compromise

Unionists people who believed the Union had to be kept together

Further Information

Books

Beller, Susan Provost. *Billy Yank and Johnny Reb: Soldiering in the Civil War*. Brookfield, CT: Twenty-first Century Books, 2000.

Rice, Earl. *Ulysses S. Grant: Defender of the Union* (Civil War Generals). Greensboro, NC: Morgan Reynolds Publishing, 2005.

Riehecky, Janet. *Ulysses S. Grant* (Encyclopedia of Presidents, Second Series). Children's Press: Danbury, CT, 2004.

Videos

Acorn Media Publications. *Civil War Legends: Ulysses S. Grant.*

CSPAN American Presidents. *Life Portrait of Ulysses S. Grant.*

———. Author's Interview Series. *Ulysses S. Grant: Soldier and President.*

PBS. American Experience: *Ulysses S. Grant, Warrior President.* 2002.

———. *The Civil War: A Film by Ken Burns.*

White Star Video. *American Legends: General U. S. Grant.* 2000.

Web Sites

Presidents of the United States

www.presidentsusa.net/grant.html

The Ulysses S. Grant home page links to countless Grant biographies, speeches, pictures, and other USG Web sites.

The White House

www.whitehouse.gov/history/presidents/ug18.html

The White House Web site features Grant's story as part of the ongoing tale of American presidents from George Washington to George W. Bush.

American Experience

www.pbs.org/wgbh/amex/grant

This highly interactive site invites you to walk in Grant's shoes as you visit his childhood or fight alongside him at Shiloh.

Bibliography

Boller, Paul F. *Presidential Campaigns*. Oxford: Oxford University Press, 1984.

Foner, Eric. *Reconstruction: America's Unfinished Revolution*. New York: Harper & Row Publishers, 1988.

Grant, Ulysses S. *Personal Memoirs of Ulysses S. Grant* (The Barnes & Noble Library of Essential Reading Series). New York: B&N Publishing, 2004.

McFeely, William S. *Grant: A Biography*. New York: Norton and Company, 1981.

Miller, Nathan. *Star-Spangled Men*. New York: Scribner, 1998.

Perret, Geoffrey. *Ulysses S. Grant: Soldier and President*. New York: Random House, 1997.

Porter, Horace. *Campaigning with Grant*. New York: Century, 1987.

Ross, Ishbel. *The General's Wife*. New York: Dodd, Mead & Company, 1959.

Simpson, Brooks D. *Ulysses S. Grant: Triumph Over Adversity, 1822–1865*. Boston: Houghton Mifflin, 2000.

Smith, Jean Edward. *Grant*. New York: Simon and Schuster, 2001.

Stiles, T. J. *Robber Barrons and Radicals*. New York: The Berkley Publishing Group, 1997.

Wilson, Edmund. *Patriotic Gore: Studies in the Literature of the American Civil War*. Oxford: Oxford University Press, 1962.

Index

About the Author

Billy Aronson's plays have been produced by Playwrights Horizons, Ensemble Studio Theatre, Wellfleet Harbor Actors Theater, and Woolly Mammoth Theatre; published in *Best American Short Plays*; and awarded a New York Foundation for the Arts grant. His writing for the musical theater includes the original concept and additional lyrics for the Broadway musical *Rent*. His TV writing includes scripts for the Cartoon Network's *Courage the Cowardly Dog*, MTV's *Beavis & Butt-Head*, Nickelodeon's *Wonder Pets* (head writer), Noggin's *Upside Down Show*, and PBS's *Postcards From Buster*, for which he received an Emmy nomination. He lives in Brooklyn with his wife, Lisa Vogel, and their children, Jake and Anna. For a good time visit www.billyaronson.com.